IRISH CINEMAS

A History in Photographs

METROPOLE
BALLROOM
CINEMA
RESTAURANT
CONTINUOUS DAILY 2 OC TO 10 50
SUNDAY 3 OC AND 8 OC
FEATURE AT 2-40 5-OC 7-15 & 9-25
CYRIL CUSACK NOEL PURCELL JIMMY ODEA PAUL FARRELL MAUREEN POTTER
IN JOHN FORD'S THE RISING OF THE MOON WITH
DENIS ODEA EILEEN CROWE MAY CRAIG AND THE ABBEY PLAYERS
REDMOND
REDMOND

IRISH CINEMAS

A History in Photographs

JIM KEENAN

Picture House Publications
2019

To Bridget and Jamie

First published in 2019 by
Picture House Publications,
5 Chesterfield Grove,
Castleknock,
Dublin
D15 XY8K
Ireland

Email: keecarto@gmail.com

ISBN 978-0-9550683-9-3

A CIP catalogue record for this book is available from the British Library.
Cover and text design by Anú Design, Tara, Co. Meath, Ireland.
Typeset by Anú Design, Tara, Co. Meath, Ireland.
Printed and bound in Malta by Gutenberg Press.

Contents

LEINSTER

MUNSTER

CONNACHT

Acknowledgements

This book would not have been possible without the assistance of many individuals and organisations. I wish to express my gratitude to the Director and staff of the National Library of Ireland; the National Photographic Archive; Dublin City Library and Archive, Dublin and Irish Collections; RTE Stills Library; Colum O'Riordan, the Irish Architectural Archive; Jim Coughlan, *Irish Examiner*; Linda O'Reilly, *Anglo-Celt*; *Belfast Telegraph*; *Irish Independent*; Libraries NI; Ulster Museum; Irish Photo Archive; Local Studies, Kilkenny Library; Waterford Museum; Donal Wylde, *The Nationalist*; David Crampton, G. & T. Crampton Ltd; the Kennelly Archive; Alamy; Old Lurgan Photos Facebook page; David Ryan, Dano Dublin Images; the Roche Collection; Karen Carty, Anú Design; Terry Foley, Anú Design.

Further thanks goes to Bridget Maher, Jamie Keenan, Michael Bolger, Frank O'Donoghue, Andy Taylor, Austin O'Brien, Joe Coleman, Sean Curtin, James Harte, Sean Kielty, Donald H. Finlay, Robin Bestick Williams, Sandra A Armstrong, Ray Flynn, Martin Flynn, Martin Whelan, Brian King, Eileen Keenan, Ann Keenan, Martin Allen, Gerard Curtis, Jörg Köster, Paula Kavanagh, Paul Gibson, Anthony Foran, Harry Havelin, James Durney, Marian Henry, Colm McNellis, John Hearne, Scott Wilson, Brendan Golden, Dan O'Shea, Alan Souter, Alec Foley, Donal Haughey, P. J. Clarke, Michael Cowhey, John Byrnes, Seamus Cafferkey, Mrs Mary Giblin, Denis North.

Preface

For much of the 20th century cinema-going was the most popular form of mass entertainment in Ireland, enjoyed by both sexes, young and old, and all social classes. At its peak in the mid-1950s, there were over 350 cinemas dotted around the island of Ireland.

An outing to the cinema was a magical experience - an opportunity to escape for a few hours into an exciting, entrancing world. But often overlooked was the important role the cinema buildings played in enhancing the cinema-going experience – particularly the 'atmospheric' cinemas with their fantasy settings. Sadly they are long gone, as indeed are most of the old cinemas. The purpose of this book is to record a selection of them before they fade from the collective memory. It illustrates the various contrasting architectural styles with examples ranging from large, luxurious Art Deco styled urban picture palaces to modest rural and suburban cinemas.

Rural cinemas played a valuable role in the social life of small town Ireland and most towns had at least one cinema. In the 1950s, even relatively small towns such as Milford, which had a population of about 550, could sustain a cinema with seating accommodation for almost 300. Unlike present-day multiplexes, which are often located on the outskirts of towns, the old rural cinemas were usually situated in the very heart of the community and frequently run by local business people. In addition, many were multifunctional and could be used for concerts, plays, public meetings, and even circuit court sittings. Their value to the community was often taken for granted and not fully appreciated until after they had closed down.

The book also contains photographs of former cinema buildings, a number of which have been sympathetically converted to other uses. Others were not so lucky and became derelict, as can be seen in several poignant images in the book. Covered in graffiti and stripped of their dignity, these once popular buildings suffered slow deaths as they lapsed into ugly eyesores. Some were left languishing in that pitiful state for years before being demolished.

The collection of illustrations has been compiled from a wide variety of sources and I am most grateful to all who have contributed photographs. In some instances, due to the absence of good quality images, I have had to resort to using poorer quality ones in order to illustrate particular cinemas. I am hopeful that this publication will help elicit additional material which could be used to produce a second volume. To that end, I would be delighted to hear from any readers who might be able to put me on the trail of further photographs.

I hope readers enjoy the book and gain some appreciation of the contribution that many of the old cinemas made to our architectural heritage.

Jim Keenan, Dublin.
August 2019

Volta Cinema, Dublin, c. 1940s. (Courtesy of the National Library of Ireland)

3904672

IRISH CINEMAS – A HISTORY IN PHOTOGRAPHS

ULSTER

★ ★ ★ ★

3904672

St. Mary's Hall, Buncrana, 1994.
(Courtesy of Colm McNellis)

Above: The former Astor Cinema, Derrybeg, 1995.
(Courtesy of Paul Gibson)

Founded by local businessman Thomas McBride and his wife Mary, the Astor in Derrybeg was the first full-time cinema to open in the Donegal Gaeltacht. When the Gael-linn film *Mise Éire* went on general release it was first screened at the Astor – a remarkable coup for a small, rural cinema. The box-office hit *Jaws* had an extended run of twelve days there in May 1977. Other popular films included *The Cardinal, The Longest Day, El Cid, One Flew Over the Cuckoo's Nest*, *ET* and *Best Seller*. The Astor opened on 20 July 1958 and closed around October 1988.

Right: Abbey Cinema, Ballyshannon, 1982.
(Courtesy of the National Library of Ireland)

The 500-seat Abbey Cinema opened on 17 November 1946. Ballyshannon Town Commissioners acquired the premises in 1989 and formed a trust to develop them as an Arts and Cultural Centre.

Strand Cinema, Strand Road, Derry, c. 1935.
(Bigger & McDonald Collection. Courtesy of LibrariesNI)

Left: Rialto Cinema, Market Street, Derry, c. 1930s.
(Bigger & McDonald Collection. Courtesy of LibrariesNI)

Right: City Cinema, William Street, Derry, c. 1930s.
(Bigger & McDonald Collection. Courtesy of LibrariesNI)

Schoolboys outside the Palace Cinema, Shipquay Street, Derry, c. 1930s. (Bigger & McDonald Collection. Courtesy of LibrariesNI)

The magician Professor John Popjie and his Radiana electric robot at the Opera House, Carlisle Road, Derry, c. 1930s.
(Bigger & McDonald Collection. Courtesy of LibrariesNI)

The 'electric robot' was merely a complicated-looking contraption with a very small woman inside it who operated the mechanical hands to perform various feats such as playing a piano or shaving a volunteer from the audience.

The Opera House auditorium, Derry.
(Bigger & McDonald Collection. Courtesy of LibrariesNI)

The Opera House opened in 1876 and showed films from about 1915. It was destroyed by fire in 1940.

Above: Midland Cinema, Waterside, Derry, c. 1935.
(Bigger & McDonald Collection. Courtesy of LibrariesNI)

Left: Midland Cinema, Waterside, Derry, c. 1931.
(Bigger & McDonald Collection. Courtesy of LibrariesNI)

Clonard Cinema, Falls Road, Belfast, c. late 1960s. (Courtesy of the Irish Architectural Archive)

Designed by William J. Moore in the Italianite style, the 1,100-seat Clonard Cinema opened on 22 December 1913. When the film *Macushla* was being shown there on 2 December 1938, a group of men in the audience stood up and threw tomatoes at the screen, completely destroying it. The preplanned incident occurred when a scene in the film showed security officers foiling an attempt to smuggle guns across the Irish border. Fights became so frequent at the cinema that the ushers resorted to carrying their own batons. The Clonard closed on 30 March 1966. It was badly damaged during the Troubles in the 1970s and was subsequently demolished.

The former Clonard Cinema, Falls Road, Belfast. (© Alamy)

Broadway Cinema, Falls Road, Belfast, 1937. (BELUM. Y3401. A.R. Hogg, © National Museums NI Collection Ulster Museum)

Designed by Thomas McLean for the Curran circuit, the 1,500-seat Broadway Cinema opened on 12 December 1936. At the end of a packed matinée performance on Easter Sunday, 24 April 1943, a group of armed men locked all the doors and took control of the cinema. The audience was instructed to be seated while a "tribute" was paid to the IRA volunteers who were killed in the 1916 Rising. In January 1972, the IRA set fire to the cinema. It did not reopen and was later demolished.

The former Broadway Cinema, Falls Road, Belfast. (© Alamy)

Picturedrome Cinema, Mountpottinger Road, Belfast, April 1935. (BELUM. Y1592. A.R. Hogg, © National Museums NI Collection Ulster Museum)

The renowned architect John McBride Neill designed the Picturedrome Cinema in the Art Deco style. The gleaming white cinema with its attractive zig-zag ornamentation and huge signage made it a very prominent building on Mountpottinger Road. The cinema, which seated 1,100, opened on 12 November 1934 with the romantic musical *Lily of Killarney*. It closed on 30 May 1970 and was demolished some years later.

Ritz Cinema, Fisherwick Place, Belfast, 1939. (BELUM. Y2221. A.R. Hogg, © National Museums NI Collection Ulster Museum)

The Ritz, promoted as 'Ireland's Wonder Cinema', opened on 9 November 1936. It was the largest and most luxurious cinema in Northern Ireland at the time. Early on the morning of 22 September 1977, incendiary bombs planted in the seats completely destroyed the interior and the roof. The cinema was reinstated and reopened in June 1981 as a four-screen multiplex. It closed on 1 July 1993 and was demolished in 1994.

Majestic Cinema, Lisburn Road, Belfast, 1936. (BELUM. Y3665. A.R. Hogg, © National Museums NI Collection Ulster Museum)

The 1,400-seat Majestic Cinema was designed by John McBride Neill and built by John Gaston. It opened on 25 May 1936 with *Curley Top*, starring Shirley Temple. The cinema closed on 4 October 1975.

Stadium Cinema, Shankill Road, Belfast, 1937. (HOYFM.BT.743, Belfast Telegraph © National Museums NI Collection Ulster Folk & Transport Museum)

Tommy Henderson, the MP for Shankill, formally opened the 1,400-seat Stadium Cinema on 16 October 1937. The opening film was *Follow the Fleet*. The cinema closed on 13 March 1976. The building was later converted into a youth and community centre.

The Lyric Cinema, High Street, Belfast, was destroyed in a German air raid on 5 May 1941. (Courtesy of the National Library of Ireland)

Opposite: The Picture House, Royal Avenue, Belfast, 1946. (Photograph reproduced courtesy of the Trustees of National Museums Northern Ireland)

NATIONAL UNION OF DISTRIBUTIVE & ALLIED WORKERS
THE PICTURE HOUSE
THE PICTURE HOUSE
THE PICTURE HOUSE
NO ENTRY
ONE WAY STREET
TO-DAY
WEDDING NIGHT
ROMANTIC INDIA
CAFE

Clockwise from top left: Gaumont Cinema, Castle Lane, Belfast. (Courtesy of the National Library of Ireland); Larne Electric Theatre, Larne. (Courtesy of the National Library of Ireland); Curzon Cinema, Ormeau Road, Belfast, c. 1979. (Courtesy of the National Library of Ireland); Tivoli Cinema, Finaghy, 1955. (Courtesy of the National Library of Ireland)

Capitol Cinema, Antrim Road, Belfast, 1943. (HOYFM.BT.739, Belfast Telegraph © National Museums NI Collection Ulster Folk & Transport Museum)

Located on the corner of the Antrim Road and Alexandra Park Avenue, the 1,000-seat Capitol Cinema opened on 9 October 1935. It was designed by Thomas McLean in the Art Deco style and featured a façade with sleek curved corners. It closed on 11 January 1975 and was later demolished. A supermarket was subsequently built on the site.

Tonic Cinema, Hamilton Road, Bangor, April 1954. (Courtesy of and © Donald H. Finlay)

The Tonic Cinema was one of the finest examples of cinema architecture in Ireland. It was designed by John McBride Neill and opened in 1936. The building also housed a ballroom, restaurant, shops and flats. It was one of just two cinemas in Northern Ireland with a Compton cinema organ – the other being the Ritz in Belfast. The 2,001-seat Tonic remained a single screen cinema throughout its lifetime. It closed in 1983 and was demolished shortly after a fire destroyed much of the building on 21 June 1992.

The former Lyric Cinema, Union Street, Lurgan, c. 1980. (Courtesy of Old Lurgan Photos Facebook Page)

Built on the site of the old Lyric Cinema, the new Lyric Cinema opened around January 1930. It was designed in a modern Renaissance style by the Belfast architect Robert Lynn. He died at an early age in 1928 and his former assistant, John McBride Neill, oversaw the project through to completion. The cinema, which was constructed of brick and faced with imitation Portland stone, seated 1,000. It was demolished in the early 1980s.

LYRIC
THEATRE Castleblayney
Showing Nightly 8.30 p.m.
SUNDAY, 14th JUNE
MATINEE AT 3 p.m.
HEATHER SEARS, ANN RYAN IN
The Black Torment
(CRIME DRAMA)
Also Ray Danton, Guy Madison in RETURN OF SANDOKAN (Adventure)
MON.
JAMES GARNER, JEAN SIMMONS IN
WOMAN WITHOUT A FACE
(SHOCK THRILLER)
Also A PLACE FOR LOVERS (Romantic)
TUES. and EVERY TUES. at 9 p.m.
BIG SPECIAL ATTRACTION
WED./THURS.
RICHARD WIDMARK, HENRY FONDA IN
MADIGAN
(ADULTS ONLY)
Big Crime . . . Big Detective Work in A Big City!
FRI./SAT.
PETER LAWFORD, IVA FRUSTENBERG IN
DEAD RUN
(CRIME THRILLER)
Also SEX AND A STRANGER (Adults Only)
Coming 21st June (For 12 Days)—WHERE EAGLES DARE
Complimentary

Above: The former Lyric Cinema, Monaghan Road, Castleblaney, 1995. (© Jim Keenan)

Right: Programme for June 1970.

The 495-seat Lyric Cinema opened around 1949. It was owned by Augustine McElroy, a local businessman who was involved in the furniture trade and the egg-producing business. The manager of the cinema was a Mr A. Muldoon.

Above: The burnt-out Magnet Cinema, Farnham Street, Cavan, 1971. (Courtesy of the Anglo-Celt)

The Magnet Cinema burned down early on Saturday morning, 11 September 1971. Twenty firemen from Cavan, Belturbet and Kileshandra fought the fire but were unable to save the building.

Right: New Magnet Cinema, Cavan, 1995. (© Jim Keenan)

Built on part of the site of the old Magnet Cinema, the new 140-seat Magnet opened on 1 September 1974 with the action drama *Enter the Dragon*, starring Bruce Lee. It operated for just over twenty years before closing in 1995.

The former Ritz Cinema, Forthill Street, Enniskillen. (Courtesy of and © Sandra A. Armstrong)

The Ritz Cinema seated 700. It was owned by John James McManus and opened in 1954 with *Snow White and the Seven Dwarfs*. The cinema closed in 1992.

Pallidrome Cinema, Railway Road, Strabane, c. 1930s. (Courtesy of the National Library of Ireland)

The Pallidrome Cinema, founded by Herbert F. Cooper and managed by Archibald Richard, was Strabane's first cinema and operated from about November 1913 to 1935. Cooper was a Londoner who came to Strabane and took over what had been Burroghs photographic business on Railway Street. Wilton and Barry took over the Pallidrome around 1931. However, when they opened their new Commodore Cinema in Strabane in 1934, they ceased showing films at the Pallidrome and converted the former cinema into a dance hall. It proved to be one of the most popular dance halls in Northern Ireland. It closed in the 1970s and the building was demolished in 2001.

Park Cinema, Dundalk, 1960.
(Courtesy of and © Paula Kavanagh)

The aftermath of the fire at the Park Cinema, Park Street, Dundalk, in February 1960. (Courtesy of and © Paula Kavanagh)

The Park Street Cinema was converted from an old bread shop and opened in 1910. The beam of light from the projector was so low that mischievous patrons could easily cast shadows on the screen with their hands. All the reels of the adventure film *Clive of India* were forcibly removed from the cinema on 7 April 1937 by two men, one armed with a revolver. The film was perceived by Republicans as glorifying British Imperialism. On 21 February 1960, a serious fire occurred at the cinema. Two units of Dundalk's fire service fought the blaze for two hours before bringing it under control. The cinema never reopened.

The former Abbey Cinema, Newry Street, Carlingford, 2016. (© Jim Keenan)

The Abbey Cinema was built by J.P. Kearney for a consortium which included himself, M. J. O'Rourke, Matt Donnelly, Donal O'Hagan and a Dr. Finegan. The name of the cinema was later changed to the Royal. One of the original directors, motor trader M.J. O'Rourke, bought out the other directors and operated the cinema for several years before putting it up for sale in the 1970s.

The former Bohemian Cinema, Tisdale Street, Ardee, 2018. (© Jim Keenan)

The Bohemian Cinema was owned by the Thorne family and opened on 30 August 1940 with *The Gang's All Here*. It was designed by the Dundalk-based architects Messrs John F. McGahon and Sons. The cinema, which seated 432, closed in 1979.

Above: Adelphi Cinema, Market Street, Dundalk, 1996. (© Jim Keenan)

Right: The Adelphi building, Dundalk, 2016. (© Jim Keenan)

The Adelphi, which seated 1,122, was the largest provincial cinema in the country when it opened on 12 May 1947. It was designed by the well-known Dublin firm of Robinson, Keefe and Devane, and built by Messrs P. McKenna and Sons, Armagh. In later years the Adelphi was subdivided into three cinemas. They closed around December 1999 and the premises were later converted into retail outlets and apartments.

Palace Cinema, Ludlow Street, Navan, 1994.
(© Jim Keenan)

The Navan Picture Palace opened on 27 February 1914. It seated 350. The principal directors of the operating company were Robert Kennedy and James Davis. Kennedy, originally from county Longford, joined the Royal Irish Constabulary as a young man where he spent most of his time as a drill instructor. He was stationed in Galway and Belfast before being transferred to Nobber where he was a sergeant in the early 1900s. He came to Navan shortly before he retired from the force in 1914. James Davis, a native of Fermoy, moved to Navan in 1887 and became a successful businessman. The Palace cinema closed from July to October 1936 to facilitate its expansion and modernisation. It reopened on 18 October with an increased seating capacity of 582. When Robert Kennedy died in 1939, his son William, headmaster at the local technical school, took over the running of the cinema. At about 6 o'clock on the evening of 9 February 1949, William Kennedy and his family suffered a dreadful tragedy. While they were having tea in their living quarters above the cinema, a fire started and spread rapidly. William Kennedy's wife and two of their children were rescued from an upstairs floor. Kennedy managed to get out of the building but went back in again to try and rescue his mother and sister. He was trapped and all three of them perished in the fire that engulfed the entire building. The fire was one of the biggest in Navan's history and could be seen from over seven miles away.

Palace Cinema, Ludlow Street, Navan, 1994. (© Jim Keenan)

The cinema was rebuilt and opened in September 1951. It was designed by Messrs J.F. McGahon and Sons, Dundalk. In 1983, it was subdivided into two smaller cinemas and the total seating capacity was reduced to 350. A big box-office hit there was *Titanic*, which played for twelve weeks. The Palace closed on 17 December 1998 and the premises were subsequently converted into a nightclub.

Left: Savoy Cinema, O'Connell Street, Dublin, 1930. (Courtesy of the Irish Architectural Archive)

Below left: Opening programme for the Savoy Cinema, Dublin.

Below right: The staff of the Savoy Cinema, Dublin. c. 1930s.

Work started on the construction of the Savoy Cinema on 18 June 1928 on a site previously occupied by the Crown and the Granville hotels, both of which were destroyed in the Civil War. Designed by the London-based architect F.C. Mitchell, it seated 2,900 and was the largest cinema in Ireland when it opened on 29 November 1929. The Savoy's stunning 'atmospheric' interior was designed to resemble a Venetian streetscape. The proscenium, which was modeled on the Rialto Bridge in Venice, framed a safety curtain painted with images of the Doge's Palace and Canale di San Marco. The film that had the longest run at the Savoy was *Educating Rita*, which ran for 14 months in 1983 and 1984. In 1969, it became Ireland's first twinned cinema when its huge single-screen auditorium was subdivided into two smaller cinemas. It was tripled in 1975, and in 1979 it became a five-screen venue. A sixth screen was added later. Screen One, which seats 700, is the country's most prestigious cinema and Irish film premières held there frequently attract national and international celebrities.

The Savoy's elaborate proscenium arch and auditorium, 1929. (Courtesy of the Irish Architectural Archive)

Left: Capitol Cinema, Prince's Street, Dublin, August 1971. (Courtesy of the National Library of Ireland)

Above: *The Four Feathers* played at the Capitol in February 1930. (Courtesy of the National Library of Ireland)

The La Scala Theatre was designed as an opera house, but it was rarely used as such and functioned mainly as a cine/variety venue. It opened on 10 August 1920. The name was changed to the Capitol when Paramount took it over in 1927. The first 'talkie' to be shown in Ireland, *The Singing Fool*, was screened there on 22 April 1929. The Capitol closed on 8 March 1972 and was demolished shortly afterwards.

Capitol Cinema, Prince's Street, Dublin, 1954.
(Courtesy of Fáilte Ireland)

Clockwise from above: Metropole Cinema, Dublin, 1971. (Courtesy of the National Library of Ireland); Liam Hughes, projectionist, Metropole, Dublin, c. 1960s; Ushers Herbie Donnelly and Laura Coates, Metropole Cinema, Dublin, c. 1960s.

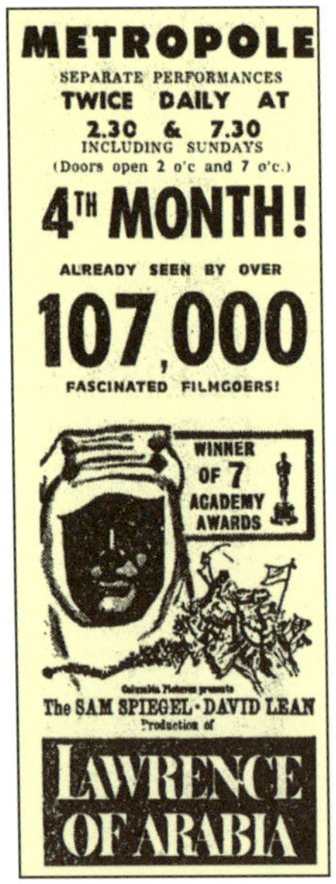

When the Rank Organisation took over the Elliman circuit in 1947, the Metropole was one of several Irish cinemas that came under its control. Rank closed the cinema for modernisation in June 1947 and the English architect Leslie Kemp was retained to redesign it. A new auditorium was constructed and the number of seats was reduced for extra comfort. A new projection box was also built. The Metropole reopened on Easter Saturday, 27 March 1948 with the award-winning film *The Best Years of Our Lives*, which ran for six months and was seen by over 280,000 people.

The most popular film shown in the Metropole Cinema was *Doctor Zhivago*, which played there for forty-three weeks (August 1966 to June 1967). Other films that had long runs there included *Mary Poppins*, *Lawrence of Arabia*, and the musical drama *Song of My Heart*. While on a family holiday in Ireland in September 1963, Prince Rainier and his wife Princess Grace attended the première of *Lawrence of Arabia* at the Metropole. The cinema closed on 11 March 1972 and was demolished in 1973.

Metropole Cinema, O'Connell Street, Dublin, 1957. (Courtesy of and © Robin Bestick Williams)

Light House Cinema, Middle Abbey Street, Dublin, 1993. (© Jim Keenan)

Light House Cinema, Dublin, September 1996. (© Jim Keenan)

The Light House Cinema opened on 11 November 1988 with Pedro Almodóvar's *Law of Desire* and Eric Rohmer's *4 Adventures of Reinette and Mirabelle*. Under the skillful stewardship of Neil Connolly and Maretta Dillon, the commercially-run arthouse made an enormous contribution to the cultural life of the city by introducing a diverse range of international films to Dublin audiences. Films shown there included *Das Boot, Au Revoir Les Enfants, Prospero's Books, Raise the Red Lantern, Salaam Bombay, Jesus of Montreal,* and the controversial Peter Greenaway film, *The Cook, The Thief, His Wife and Her Lover.* One of the most commercially successful films to play there was Thaddeus O'Sullivan's *December Bride*, which ran for ten weeks when it was released in 1990. The cinema closed on 28 September 1996 and was demolished in 1999.

Top left: Staff of the Regent Cinema, Dublin, on opening night 18 May 1967. (Courtesy of Gertie Carson)

Top right: The former Regent Cinema, Findlater Place, Dublin. (© Jim Keenan)

Bottom left: Cameo Cinema, Middle Abbey Street, Dublin, September 1976. (© RTE Stills Library)

Bottom right: The former Cameo Cinema, Dublin, 1995. (© Jim Keenan)

In 1987, loyalist terrorists attempted to firebomb the Cameo using an incendiary device. The cinema opened on 30 July 1976 and closed on 15 March 1990.

The Adelphi Cinema was built on the site of the old Plaza ballroom and restaurant which burnt down in 1935. The cinema opened on 12 January 1939 with *The Adventures of Robin Hood* starring Errol Flynn as the eponymous hero. It was designed by ABC's staff architect, William Riddell Glen, in association with local Irish architect Robert Donnelly, and built by Messrs E. Stone and Sons. The façade was clad in Portland stone and the overall design of the cinema resembled an intermediate stage between the Classical and Modern architectural styles. The auditorium, which seated a total of 2,325 patrons, accommodated 1,553 in the parterre and 772 in the balcony. Double staircases led from the foyer to the circle and the balcony restaurant. At mezzanine level, the restaurant looked down on the lobby on four sides. Almost four miles of carpeting was used to carpet the cinema. When EMI gained control of the cinema in the late 1960s, they decided to subdivide it into three smaller cinemas. President Éamon de Valera was invited to perform the official opening of the new three-screen Adelphi in October 1970. However, the President felt it would demean the dignity of his office and declined the invitation with a curt reply: 'If I opened it, I'd be opening every chicken coup in Ireland'. The Adelphi closed on 30 November 1995.

Adelphi Cinema, Middle Abbey Street, Dublin, 1993. (© Jim Keenan)

Top: Academy Cinema, Pearse Street, Dublin, 1967. (© RTE Stills Library) **Left:** The former Academy Cinema, Dublin, deteriorated rapidly after part of the building was destroyed by fire in March 1994. (© Jim Keenan). **Right:** The premises were converted into offices in 2007. (© Jim Keenan)

Grafton Cinema,Grafton Street, Dublin.
27 November 1955.
(irishphotoarchive.ie/Lensmen Collection)

Mary Street Cinema, Dublin, December 1953. (Courtesy of Dublin City Library and Archive: Dublin and Irish Collections)

The Mary Street Cinema, situated on the corner of Mary Street and Wolfe Tone Street, was founded by John J. Farrell and opened on 19 December 1912. It was designed by George Luke O'Connor. The auditorium had panelled recessed walls, decorative arches and a richly embellished carved ceiling. The 'Maro', as it was commonly known, was a low-grade cinema that generally showed older films. It was designed to accommodate 920 patrons, but many more were regularly packed in. It attracted a rough element, and gang warfare frequently broke out inside and outside the premises. The cinema closed on 11 January 1959. The closing films were *Baby Face Nelson* and *Price of Greed*.

Mary Street Cinema, Dublin, early 1950s. (© RTE Stills Library)

Left: Astor Cinema, Eden Quay, Dublin, 1971. (Courtesy of the National Library of Ireland)

Bottom right: Staff of the Astor Cinema, Dublin, 1969. (Courtesy of Oliver Allen)

In the 1950s, when Tommy Gogan was manager of the Astor Cinema, it specialised in showing foreign-language films. Gogan's love of grand opera was reflected in his choice of films shown there, which included *The Barber of Seville*, *Aida* and *Tosca*. In later years, however, the programming became erratic with product alternating between soft porn and arthouse. In March 1984, it showed the satirical comedy *Polyester*. The film became known for its use of 'Odorama', a gimmick that allowed audiences to smell the odours that corresponded with the images they saw on the screen. Before entering the auditorium, patrons were given numbered 'scratch-and-sniff' cards which gave off an odour when scratched. During the course of the film, cue numbers would appear in the corner of the screen indicating which number to scratch. Known as 'smellies' in the cinema trade, 'Odorama' and similar processes soon died out when the novelty wore off. *Polyester* got poor reviews when it was shown at the Astor and only ran for a week.

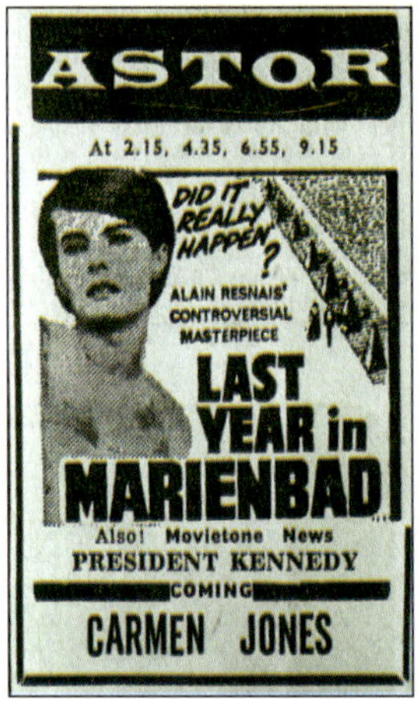

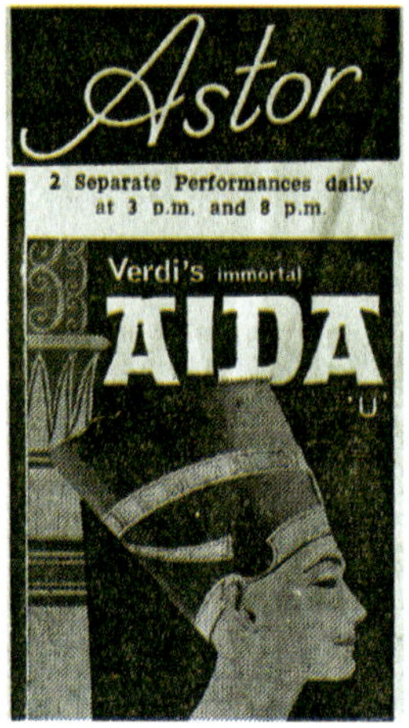

Carlton Cinema, O'Connell Street, Dublin, 1964. (Courtesy of Anthony Foran)

Designed by the Dublin firm of Robinson and Keefe, the 2,000-seat Carlton Cinema opened on 16 April 1938 with the romantic comedy *The Awful Truth*. When Martin Scorsese's controversial film *The Last Temptation of Christ* was shown there on 11 November 1988, twenty people protested outside the cinema at its first public screening. The Carlton closed on 20 October 1994.

Left: The former Camden Cinema, Camden Street, Dublin, c. late 1940s. (Courtesy of the National Library of Ireland)

The 400-seat Camden Cinema opened on 25 October 1912 with the Italian film *Dante's Inferno*. It was founded by Alfred Henry Poulter, a retired stockbroker. The premises had previously consisted of a drapery on the ground floor, living accommodation on the upper floors, and a cottage at the rear. The renowned architect Rudolph Maximillian Butler designed the cinema, but it had a most unsatisfactory layout. Patrons entered the auditorium through a door beneath the screen and were immediately struck and dazzled by the beam of light from the projector. Poulter's association with the Camden lasted just over twelve years. He died of pneumonia on 29 March 1925. His wife, Wilhelmina Georgina, who lived above the cinema, died less than a year later. In the 1940s, Odeon (Ireland) took over the Camden and ran it until it closed on 28 August 1948.

Camden Cinema, c. 1910s.

Ernest Gébler worked as a projectionist at the Camden Cinema before he became a well-known author. While the films were running, he would often spend his time in the projection box writing articles, short stories and novels.

Left: The old Stella Cinema, Rathmines Road, Dublin, May 1996. (© Jim Keenan)

The businessman Anthony O'Grady was instrumental in setting up the Stella Cinema in Rathmines. It opened on 29 January 1923 and had seating for almost 1,000. During the intervals between film performances, multicoloured lights illuminated a beautiful water fountain situated in front of the screen. In the 1970s, the Stella hosted a series of music concerts. Three generations of the O'Grady family ran the cinema for just over eighty years before it closed in August 2004.

Right: The new Stella Cinema, Rathmines Road, Dublin, 2018. (© Jim Keenan)

The old Stella Cinema lay unused for many years before being beautifully restored. The premises reopened in October 2017 and now house a cinema, a restaurant and a bar.

Classic Cinema, Rathfarnham Road, Terenure, Dublin, 7 August 1959.
(Courtesy of the National Library of Ireland)

Built on the site formerly occupied by the Blessington tram terminus, the 750-seat Classic Cinema opened on 1 July 1938. In 1964, when Albert Kelly took over as general manager of the Kenilworth and Classic cinemas, he decided to run the Classic as an arthouse cinema. The cinema showed Continental films as well as seasons of ballet and opera films. In later years it reverted to showing mainstream films. It closed on 19 June 1976.

Classic Cinema, Harold's Cross, Dublin, 13 September 1992. (© Jim Keenan)

The Classic was renowned for its midnight screenings of the cult film *The Rocky Horror Picture Show*. The 'audience participation' film was screened on Friday and Saturday nights for twenty-two years, and attracted people from all over Dublin. One regular patron was reputed to have seen the film over 800 times. The Classic closed on 28 August 2003 and was demolished in 2007.

Above: The former Forum Theatre, Serpentine Avenue, Ballsbridge, Dublin, 15 April 1995. (© Jim Keenan) **Left:** The former cinema is now a Sikh temple, 2019. (© Jim Keenan)

The former Oscar Theatre, Serpentine Avenue, Ballsbridge, c. mid-1980s. (Image David Ryan courtesy Dano Dublin Images)

James F. O'Neill, bought the old Assembly Rooms at Serpentine Avenue in 1912 and adapted it for use as a cinema. Operating a hand-cranked projector, O'Neill screened the films himself. Percy W. Whittle took over the cinema and changed the name to the Ritz, but locals always called it by its nickname, 'The Shack'. Whittle ran the cinema for several years before selling it on to George Jay in October 1949. The Ritz closed around September 1973. The name was changed to the Oscar and the cinema reopened on 18 October 1973. It only lasted a few years and closed on 27 November 1976. The building was subsequently converted into a 284-seat theatre. Unfortunately, it was beset by financial difficulties and the building was put up for sale in 1984. It was sold in December 1986 and converted into a Sikh temple.

The former Apollo Cinema, Walkinstown, Dublin, 1992. (© Jim Keenan)

The former Leinster Cinema, Dolphin's Barn, Dublin, 1995. (© Jim Keenan)

Situated at the junction of Cork Street and Ruben Street, the Leinster Cinema opened on 3 November 1936. It seated 1,250 and was designed in the Art Deco style by the firm of Robinson and Keefe. On Saturday afternoons at the fourpenny rush, one of the ushers was renowned for barking orders while swinging his belt through the air for dramatic effect. The cinema closed on 18 May 1968 and was later converted into Ireland's first indoor ice skating rink. The building was demolished in October 2004 and apartments were built on the site.

Pavilion Cinema, Marine Road, Dún Laoghaire, Co. Dublin, 1976. (© RTE Stills Library)

When a fire destroyed the Pavilion Cinema on 10 November 1940, troops had to shatter the locks on the projection box with rifle fire to gain access and save films and other valuable material. The cinema was rebuilt and opened on Easter Saturday, 12 April 1941. It closed on 29 June 1974 and was put up for sale. Dún Laoghaire Rathdown county council purchased the premises and used them as a theatre and occasional cinema until 1984. They lay unused for fifteen years before being demolished in the late 1990s. An apartment complex and the new Pavilion Theatre were later built on the site.

Ormonde Cinema, Lower Kilmacud Road, Stillorgan, Co. Dublin, July 1976. (© RTE Stills Library)

The 1,000-seat Ormonde Cinema, which opened in August 1954, cost about £40,000 to build. It was designed by W.A. Maguire for John J. Kavanagh. The cinema had an unusual curved canopy and a frontage faced with Howth stone. It closed on 30 July 1978 and was later demolished.

Forum Cinema, Glasthule, Co. Dublin, 28 July 1999. (© Jim Keenan)

In 1971, Barney O'Reilly, a well-known figure in the Irish cinema trade, purchased what had at one time been the old Astoria Cinema in Glasthule. After renovating the building, he relaunched it as the Forum Cinema and installed the first automated projection facilities in Ireland. However, this resulted in a dispute between him and the Irish Transport and General Workers Union, which represented projectionists. O'Reilly locked himself inside the cinema and went on hunger strike 'to establish his constitutional right to employ non-union labour'. He continued his protest for five days, but stopped after being advised by a doctor to do so. He reached an agreement with the trade union and his cinema reopened on 6 December 1971 as a union house. It closed on 3 September 1999 and was demolished in August 2002.

Gala Cinema, Ballyfermot, Dublin, c. mid-1950s.
(Courtesy of George Crampton, G. & T. Crampton Ltd)

Built by Messrs G & T Crampton in sixteen months, this massive suburban cinema was formally opened by the parish priest of Ballyfermot, the Rev. Michael Troy, on 23 November 1955. It opened with the musical *Lucky Me*. The cinema, which was owned and operated by Republic Pictures, was designed by J.F. McCormack and seated 1,850. It closed in 1980.

Plaza Cinema, Finglas, Dublin, June 1993.
(© Jim Keenan)

Finglas was without a cinema from when the old Casino closed in 1970 until the Plaza Cinema opened at the Janelle Shopping Centre in 1989. The new cinema opened on 29 June with a total seating capacity of 360. The first films shown there were *Twins* and *The Accused*. The Plaza had a short lifespan and closed around 1996. It was later demolished.

Casino Cinema, McKee Avenue, Finglas, Dublin, 1967. (© RTE Stills Library)

Designed by John E. Collins and built by Messrs Maher and Murphy, the Casino opened on 25 November 1955 with a seating capacity of 1,910. It closed on 26 September 1970. Fergal Quinn bought the building and merged it with his supermarket next door.

Fountain Cinema, James's Street, Dublin, c.1950s. (Courtesy of the Irish Architectural Archive)

The Fountain Cinema (aka 'The Bowery') lived up to its nickname. It was ventilated by a series of electric pumps. Unfortunately, they weren't powerful enough to cope with the foul smells at the packed matinées when some of the children urinated on the floor of the auditorium. They did this partly because they feared other children would take their seats if they left them to use the toilets. The ushers sprayed disinfectant into the air over the audience to try and counteract the odours. The cinema opened on 26 February 1923 and closed on 23 June 1962.

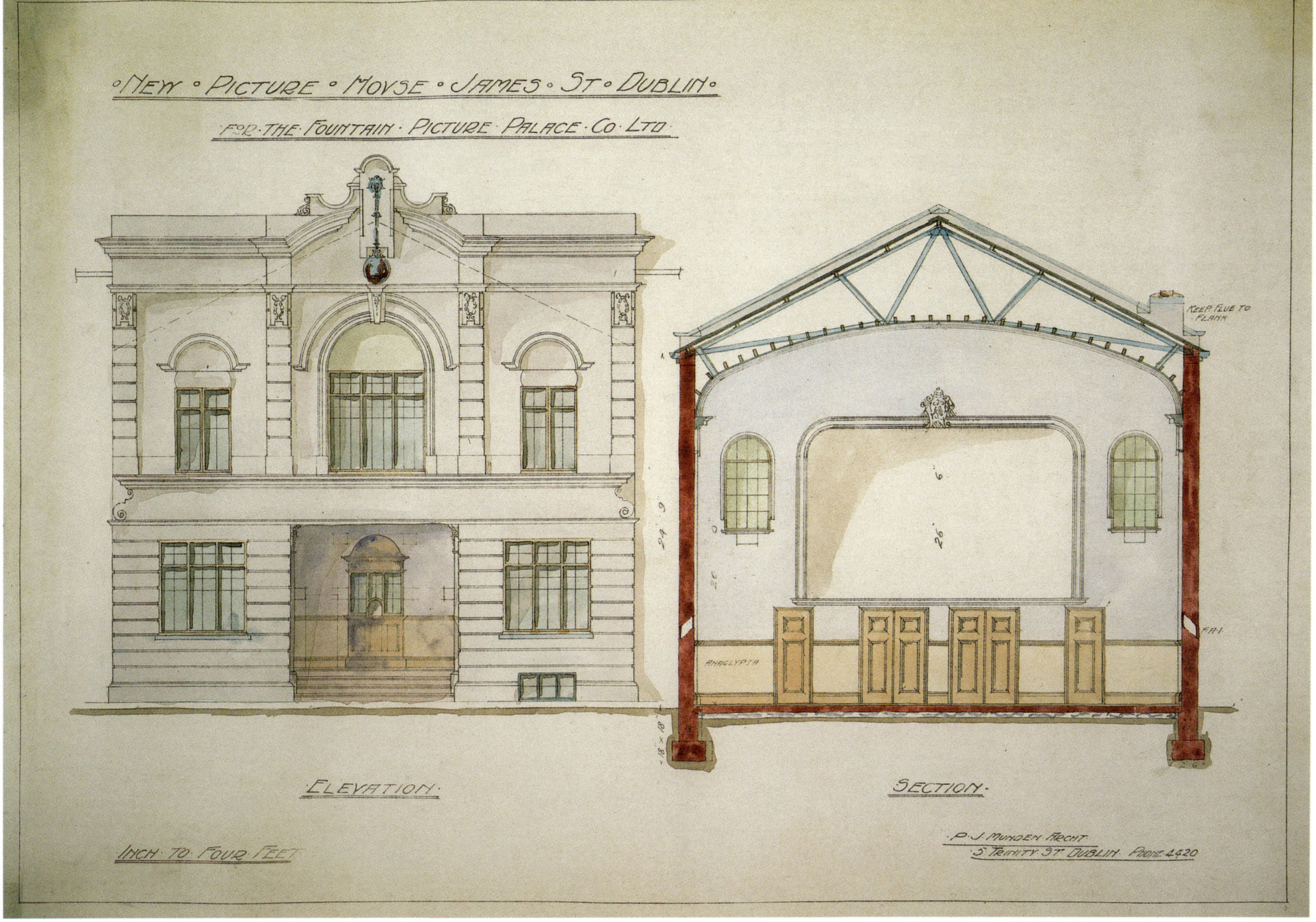

The initial architectural plans for the Fountain Cinema, Dublin. (Courtesy of the Irish Architectural Archive)

The early architectural plans for the cinema show a two-storey above street level structure. However, they must have been revised because the finished building turned out to be a three-storey structure.

Phibsboro Cinema, North Circular Road, Dublin, 1953. (irishphotoarchive.ie/Lensmen Collection)

Aubrey Vincent O'Rourke designed the 500-seat Phibsboro Cinema. It opened in May 1914 and was embroiled in controversy just a few weeks later when it showed the film *In the Shadow of a Throne* on 4 June. Twin brothers William and Francis Larkin stood up in the audience and protested against the showing of the film by shouting and throwing ink at the screen. The cinema closed on 25 January 1953 and was demolished to provide a site for the new State Cinema.

Bohemian Cinema, Phibsboro Road, Dublin, 1974. (Courtesy of and © Harry Havelin)

Frederick Arthur Sparling opened his Bohemian Cinema on 8 June 1914. A former medical student at Trinity College, Dublin, he was descended from a well-known Cromwellian family in Scariff. Sparling was just twenty-three years old when he embarked on a career in the cinema business. A serious fire destroyed the Bohemian on 24 October 1927 and ended his association with the cinema. Sparling left Ireland with his wife and children and moved to Worthington, Sussex, where he died in 1934 from pneumonia at the early age of forty-three. John George McEntagart and John Flood bought the gutted Bohemian Cinema and had it rebuilt. They opened it under new management on 17 March 1931. The Bohemian was purchased by developers in 1973, but closed soon afterwards on 30 March 1974. It was demolished some years later.

Phoenix Cinema, Ellis Quay, Dublin, 1952.
(irishphotoarchive.ie/Lensmen Collection)

Formally known as 'The Phoenix Picture Palace', the 'Feeno' (as it was commonly known) was anything but palatial. In fact, it was one of the toughest and most primitive cinemas in the city. Designed by Francis Bergin, it was Dublin's first purpose-built cinema. Ushers, brandishing canes, wielded them mercilessly to keep order in the children's queues. When being interviewed for an usher's job at the cinema, candidates were often asked if they could swim. The question was posed because the management knew (from past experience) that ushers were quite likely to end up in the nearby River Liffey during the course of one of the many fights that occurred there. When a film performance ended, unruly patrons frequently vented their resentment by throwing detritus at the screen. In order to protect the screen, one of the projectionists had to position himself at the side of the proscenium and manually lower the safety curtain just before 'The End' credit appeared. If timed properly, the safety curtain took the brunt of assorted missiles that were intended for the screen. (The much-abused safety curtain featured a lady sitting on a park stool playing a harp). The Phoenix closed in 1960.

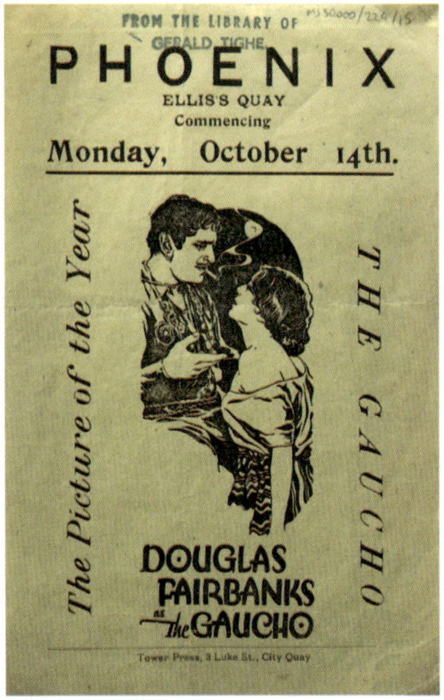

(Courtesy of the National Library of Ireland)

THE REGAL
GENTS HAIRDRESSING
PHOENIX CINEMA
SAILOR BEWARE
STATION
HOUSE

Workmen involved in building the Drumcondra Cinema, 1935. (Courtesy of the National Library of Ireland)

Drumcondra Cinema, Dublin, 1935 (Courtesy of the National Library of Ireland)

Designed by Henry J. Lyons for the Ging circuit, the Drumcondra Grand Cinema opened on 19 October 1934. It seated 1,200. The cinema closed on 24 March 1968 and the building was subsequently converted into a supermarket.

The former Grove Panoramic Cinema, Lucan, 1993. (© Jim Keenan)

Danny J. O'Leary and Ronald Rice built the Premier Cinema at the junction of Lucan Bridge and Main Street and opened it on 7 February 1945. The cinema, which was designed by A.A. Murphy, seated 290. The Ward family bought it in 1955 and the name was changed to the Grove Panoramic. It closed in the 1980s and lay derelict for many years before being demolished in the 1990s.

Savoy Cinema, Dublin Street, Balbriggan, Co. Dublin, 1971. (Courtesy of the National Library of Ireland)

Mr. D.J. Donovan, Dublin's County Commissioner, formally opened the Savoy Cinema on 19 December 1944. The Art Deco cinema, which seated 800, was completed in ten months by local builder J.J. Walsh. The Savoy closed in June 1974, but reopened as the Europa Cinema on 9 August 1974 under the stewardship of Kevin and Adrian Cunningham. The cinema closed permanently around early 1981. The frontage is a protected structure.

Abbey Cinema, Wentworth Place, Wicklow, 1994.
(© Jim Keenan)

This unusual-looking cinema, which featured a façade with crenallated towers, opened on 21 May 1942. In later years the 660-seat single-screen auditorium was subdivided into two smaller cinemas, both of which closed in early 2002 because of poor attendance. Later that year it was vandalised beyond repair. In July 2005, in an apparent arson attack, the building was set alight. It became derelict over the following years and was demolished in November 2012.

Abbey Cinema, Wentworth Place, Wicklow, 1994.(© Jim Keenan)

Royal Cinema, Quinnsboro Road, Bray, October 1973. (Courtesy of the National Library of Ireland)

The then Minister of Agriculture, Dr. J. Ryan, opened the 1,000-seat Royal Cinema on 26 December 1935. It was designed by Vincent Kelly and built by Messrs McNally and Company, East Wall, Dublin. The cinema closed in 2007.

Above: Ormonde Cinema, Victoria Road, Greystones, 1994. (© Jim Keenan)

Left: The former Ormonde Cinema, Greystones, 2014. (© Jim Keenan)

Some memorable scenes from the first series of the television sitcom *Father Ted* were filmed at the Ormonde. In the third episode, Fathers Ted Crilly and Dougall Maguire are shown holding placards proclaiming 'Down with this sort of Thing' while protesting outside the cinema against the showing of the controversial film *The Passion of Saint Tibulus*. The Ormonde closed in 2007.

Ormonde Cinema, Upper Main Street, Arklow, 1994. (© Jim Keenan)

In the mid-1930s, James J. Kavanagh and his brother purchased the site of the old Royal Irish Constabulary barracks with the intention of building a cinema and dance hall on it. The local parish priest objected to the development because of its proximity to the Catholic church, which stood directly opposite the site. Despite his objections, construction went ahead and the 600-seat Ormonde Cinema opened around 1938. It closed in the early 1980s, but in 1988 the Ward Anderson group reopened it as a two-screen cinema. It closed in 2003.

Above: The former Abbey Cinema, Lower George's Street, Wexford, 1993. (© Jim Keenan)

Named after the nearby 12th century Selskar Abbey, the Abbey Cinema opened on 20 January 1947 with *The Seventh Veil*. The cinema cost £21,511 to construct and seated 1,200. It closed quietly on 10 September 1992 with only fifteen people in the audience watching the closing film *Far and Away*. The photograph (above) shows it in a sad state shortly before it was demolished.

Left: Ritz Cinema, New Ross. (Courtesy of Denis North)

Above: Dara Cinema, Main Street, Naas, February 1994. (© Jim Keenan)

Right: The former Dara Cinema, Naas, 2016. (© Jim Keenan)

COLISEUM CINEMA, NAAS.

OPENING ANNOUNCEMENT

Friday, February 9th. Doors Open, 7.30 p.m. Commencing 8 o'clock, sharp.

The year's funniest comedy played by the Screen's greatest stars.

GINGER ROGERS and DAVID NIVEN in

BACHELOR MOTHER

With Charles Coburn and Frank Albertson.

A laugh at life, a look at love and a deep romance to provide the funniest screen

The Dara was originally called the Coliseum Cinema, which opened on 9 February 1940 with *Bachelor Mother*, starring Ginger Rogers and David Niven. The 750-seat cinema was built and operated by the Kelly/Egan circuit. The Dara closed on 8 February 2007. The last films shown there were *Goal 2* and *Infamous*.

Above: Oscar Cinemas, Henry Street, Newbridge, 1994. (© Jim Keenan)

Right: The former Oscar Cinemas, Newbridge, 2016. (© Jim Keenan)

The 400-seat Oscar Cinema was converted from the old Palace Cinema and relaunched in October 1973 by Paddy Melia's Modern Irish Theatres Company. The film *Braveheart*, some of which was filmed nearby on the Curragh plains, had a six-week run there and played to packed houses. The Oscar closed on 12 January 2006.

Above: Curragh Picture House, Curragh Military Camp, c. 1918.

One of two cinemas located in the Curragh Military Camp, the 750-seat Curragh Picture House opened around 1915. It was operated by David Frame and Christopher Sylvester Carr. The cinema closed in 1982 and the building was destroyed in a fire in 1989.

Right: Tower Cinema, Kildare, c. 1940s. (Courtesy of James Durney)

The 800-seat Tower Cinema opened on 1 December 1942. In 1974, it was relaunched as the Studio One Cinema. It closed in 1987.

The former Grove Cinema, Leinster Street, Athy, 1994. (© Jim Keenan)

The most popular film shown at the Grove Cinema was *Jurassic Park*, which ran for six weeks. The 1,000-seat cinema, designed by William Dwyer and built by George Nash, opened on 24 August 1956 with *There's no Business Like Show Business*. The Grove closed after being vandalised and set on fire in November 1992. It reopened for a short while before finally closing on 30 December 1993. The building was demolished in January 2004.

The former Astor Cinema, Kilree Street, Bagenalstown, 1994. (© Jim Keenan)

The proprietor of the Astor, Henry Godfrey Brown, was convicted in July 1955 of abstracting electricity from the E.S.B. to run his cinema over an eleven-year period between 1940 and 1951. He was sentenced to six months in prison. In the 1950s, it became an annual tradition for the townspeople to gather outside the Astor to ring in the New Year with musical entertainment provided courtesy of the management of the cinema. The Astor closed on 31 August 1980.

Grand Central Cinema, Tullow, 1990. (Courtesy of Ray and Martin Flynn)

Tom Flynn opened his Grand Central Cinema, Tullow, on 2 May 1940. It operated for fifty years before closing on 24 June 1990.

Coliseum Cinema, Upper Tullow Street, Carlow, 1993. (© Jim Keenan)

The 750-seat Coliseum Cinema was designed by Thomas Burke and opened on 19 September 1941 with the comedy film *Bachelor Mother*. The cinema closed in 1994 and was demolished shortly afterwards.

Regent Cinema, William Street, Kilkenny, c. 1990s.
(© Jim Keenan)

The Regent Cinema opened on 18 April 1947. It seated 1,100. During the course of its construction five workmen were seriously injured when scaffolding gave way. The film *Lock Up All Your Daughters,* which was filmed in Kilkenny, had its Irish première at the Regent in 1969. Other popular films shown there were *Jurassic Park* and *Titanic*. The Dubliners, Planxty, and Christy Moore were just some of the many performers who performed at the cinema. It closed on 9 August 1998 and was put up for sale in December 2000. The former cinema was demolished and Regent House, a rehabilitation centre, was built on the site.

The former Odeon Cinema, Bohercrussia Street, Freshford, 2017.
(© Jim Keenan)

The Odeon Cinema opened on 7 December 1944. It was designed by Captain Cecil W. Buggy and built by the Kilkenny contractor Edward Nolan. The cinema attracted almost 600 patrons on the opening night. To celebrate the occasion, a select number of guests were treated to dinner in the cinema after the first film performance.

Savoy Cinema, Parliament Street, Kilkenny, 1970. (Courtesy of Local Studies, Kilkenny County Libraries)

The Savoy Cinema opened on the 23 November 1936. It was designed by a Mr. T. Kelly and seated 850. It closed in 1985. The last film shown there was *Ghostbusters*. Kilkenny Corporation purchased the building with assistance from the Arts Council and, after undergoing major alterations, it reopened in 1993 as the Watergate Theatre.

Left: Coliseum Cinema, Bull Lane, Portlaoise, 1994. (© Jim Keenan)

Below left: The former Coliseum Cinema, New Road, Abbeyleix, 2018. (© Jim Keenan)

Below right: Two boys flanking an advertisement board outside the Coliseum Cinema, Abbeyleix, 1948. (Courtesy of Martin Whelan)

The Coliseum Cinema seated 600 and opened on 1 November 1944. It closed in 1966 and was sold to a local businessman who reopened it as the Milo Cinema in January 1967. The cinema closed in the early 1970s.

The former Savoy Cinema, Market Square, Portarlington, 1994. (© Jim Keenan)

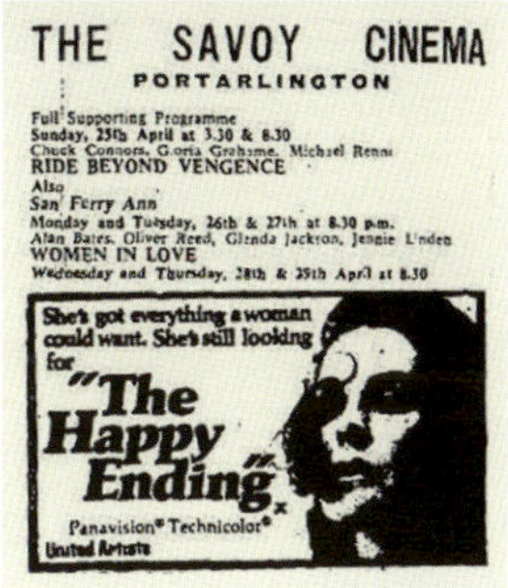

THE SAVOY CINEMA
PORTARLINGTON

Full Supporting Programme
Sunday, 25th April at 3.30 & 8.30
Chuck Connors, Gloria Grahame, Michael Rennie
RIDE BEYOND VENGENCE
Also
San Ferry Ann
Monday and Tuesday, 26th & 27th at 8.30 p.m.
Alan Bates, Oliver Reed, Glenda Jackson, Jennie Linden
WOMEN IN LOVE
Wednesday and Thursday, 28th & 29th April at 8.30

She's got everything a woman could want. She's still looking for "The Happy Ending" X
Panavision® Technicolor®
United Artists

The Savoy Cinema opened on 21 November 1944 and closed in the early 1990s. It seated 800. The former cinema featured in the 1992 film *Into the West*. One scene showed two boys on a white horse galloping out through the front doors of the cinema.

Left: The former Grand Central Cinema, Market Square, Tullamore, 1994. (© Jim Keenan) **Right:** Grand Central Cinema, Tullamore, c. 1978.

Left: Savoy Cinema, Tara Street, Tullamore, 1994. (© Jim Keenan) **Right:** The Savoy Cinema, Tullamore, opened in February 1983. It had previously been used as a dance hall.

Savoy, O'Connell Square,
Edenderry, 1994.
(© Jim Keenan)

The Roscrea and Athy Picture Company opened their Savoy Cinema in Edenderry in 1944. It was later taken over by Eugene John Paul O'Brien, a well-known businessman in Edenderry. The most popular film shown at the Savoy was *Eat the Peach*, which was filmed in nearby Allenwood. It played at the Savoy for three weeks. The cinema closed around 1994 and lay unused for many years before being demolished.

The playwright and screenwriter Eugene O'Brien, whose father owned the cinema, wrote a play called *Savoy*, which was set in a provincial cinema on the night it closes down. In the play, the manager, his son, and the projectionist reminisce about the years they spent at the cinema and ponder their futures.

Ritz Cinema, Custume Place, Athlone, 1985. (© RTE Stills Library)

Designed by William O'Dwyer and Michael Scott and Associates, the Ritz Cinema was a wonderful example of cinema architecture built in the International style. Unfortunately, some of the features in the original plans were never incorporated into the finished building. The impressive fenestrated façade was substantially altered in later years, much to its detriment. The cinema opened on 14 February 1940 and was demolished in December 1999.

Left: Adelphi Cinema, Gleeson Street, Athlone, 1971. (Courtesy of the National Library of Ireland) **Right:** The former Adelphi Cinema, Athlone, 2017. (© Jim Keenan)

Left: Ritz Cinema, Castle Street, Mullingar, 1995. (© Jim Keenan)

Below right: Ritz Cinema, Castle Street, Mullingar, 1995. (© Jim Keenan)

Below left: The Hibernian Cinema and adjacent buildings, Mullingar, c. 1950s. (The name of the cinema was changed to the Ritz in 1989).

Auburn Hall, Main Street, Edgeworthstown, c. 1990s. (Courtesy of Marian Henry)

The Auburn Hall opened on 18 January 1946 as a dance hall and on 21 April that year it opened as a cinema. The first film shown there was *Can't Help Singing*. The hall was named after the village of Auburn, which many will remember from Goldsmith's poem 'The Deserted Village'. The hall was also used for concerts, variety shows, bingo and circuit court sessions.

The former Alpha Cinema, Barrack Street, Granard, 1995. (© Jim Keenan)

Local solicitor Alan McDonald and his wife Alice founded the Alpha Cinema, the first permanent cinema building in Granard. It seated 350 and opened on 6 June 1946 with *The Santa Fe Trail*. The cinema operated until about 1967. The building now functions as a community centre.

Top: Odeon Cinema and surroundings, Longford, 1995. (© Jim Keenan)

Bottom: Odeon Cinema, Bridge Street, Longford, 1995. (© Jim Keenan)

Built on the site of the former Foresters Hall, the Odeon Cinema opened on 9 October 1941 with *Spring Parade*. A fire which occurred there on 12 March 1950 destroyed the auditorium. The cinema was rebuilt. In 1981, the Ward Anderson group purchased the single-screen cinema and subdivided it into two smaller cinemas. The most popular films shown there were *ET* and *Three Men and a Little Lady*. The Odeon closed on 25 May 1997. The cinema was later demolished and a multiplex was built on the site.

IRISH CINEMAS – A HISTORY IN PHOTOGRAPHS

MUNSTER

★★★★

Savoy Cinema, Waterford, c. 1948.
(Courtesy of John Hearne)

Savoy Cinema, Broad Street, Waterford, 1956. (Courtesy of Waterford Museum)

Local building contractors Messrs John Hearne and Son started work on the construction of the new Savoy Cinema on Broad Street in early October 1936. It opened fourteen months later on 13 December 1937 with the romantic musical *Rose Marie*. Designed by the well-known firm of Robinson and Keefe, the cinema seated 1,200 and was built on the site of the old Broad Street Cinema. The Savoy was undoubtedly the most comfortable and luxurious cinema in Waterford. It also had a fine restaurant. The cinema closed in September 1976. For a short while afterwards it was used as an entertainment centre. The cinema's former auditorium now houses a bookshop.

Left: O'Brien's Cinema, Barrack Street, Tallow. (Courtesy of Austin O'Brien)

In 1924, Dave Sheehan and his son built O'Brien's Hall in Tallow for local businessman Dan O'Brien, who ran a garage business adjacent to it. The hall was constructed as a dance hall and theatre, but was later converted into a 500-seat cinema. In 1949, it was purchased by Sean Hyde from Fermoy. He renamed it the Regal Cinema. In 1974, the O'Brien family bought it back again. The cinema closed in 1975 and was demolished to provide a site for an extension to the family motor and garage business.

Below left: Workmen who built the 700-seat Rex Cinema, Tramore, photographed in front of the building. (Courtesy of Andy Taylor)

Below right: Rex Cinema, Tramore, 1971. (Courtesy of the National Library of Ireland)

The Rex Cinema opened on 24 September 1945 and closed on 19 December 1977.

Above: Ormonde Cinema, O'Connell Street, Dungarvan, October 2002. (© Jim Keenan)
Left: Usher Jimmy Whelan, Ormonde Cinema, Dungarvan. (Courtesy of Waterford County Museum)

The Ormonde Cinema opened on 11 April 1945. It cost £20,000 to construct and was owned and operated by local businessman Daniel J. Crotty and film proprietor James J. Kavanagh. The façade of the 1,000-seat cinema featured a triptych of stained glass depicting a sun burst. The first manager was William Spencer from Templemichael. In later years the Ormonde was taken over by the Ward Anderson group. In 2001, it was converted into a two-screen venue with seating for 279 patrons. The cinema closed in September 2005 and was demolished on 29 March 2014. Social housing was subsequently built on the site.

Ritz Cinema, Washington Street, Cork, c. 1975. (Courtesy of the Irish Examiner Archive)

Built on the site of the old Washington Cinema, which burned down in 1938, the 590-seat Ritz Cinema opened on 13 August 1939 with the historical drama *Suez*. The original proprietors were Stephen F. Whelan, a qualified chemist, and Thomas Meaghar, a solicitor. Amalgamated Cinemas (Ireland) Ltd took over the cinema in August 1966 and ran it until it closed in February 1974. It was relaunched as the Classic Cinema on 28 December 1975. The cinema failed to do good business and was sold to Abbey films in 1979. It closed on 10 August 1989 and was later demolished.

Savoy Cinema, Patrick Street, Cork, 25 May 1956. (Courtesy of the Irish Examiner Archive)

Work started on the construction of the Savoy Cinema in September 1931 and approximately 1,000 people were employed on the site over the seven months it took to build the cinema. The Lord Mayor of Cork, Frank J. Daly, performed the opening ceremony on 12 May 1932. The first film shown there was the romantic comedy *Peach O'Reno*. Designed by the Bradford architectural firm of Messrs Moore and Crabtree, and built by Messrs Meagher and Hayes, it cost £148,000 to construct and was the largest cinema in Cork with seating for 2,242. Internally and externally, the cinema was hugely impressive but lacked a unity of style. The magnificent Art Deco façade, executed in Hathern faience, contrasted starkly with the ornate 'atmospheric' auditorium, which, like the Savoy in Dublin, was designed to resemble a street scene in Venice. The Savoy hosted the first ever Cork Film Festival in 1956 and every year thereafter until 1975. The festival was a huge success and attracted film stars, producers and directors to the city for the event. Fred Bridgman was the resident organist there for thirty years until he retired in 1967. Particularly successful films shown at the cinema included *Goldfinger* and *Mary Poppins*. The Savoy was also used as a venue for concerts and among the many who appeared there were Gracie Fields, Paul Robeson, Tom Jones, the Bee Gees, and the Rolling Stones. The cinema closed on 1 February 1975. The last film shown there was *Towering Inferno*.

The auditorium and proscenium of the Savoy Cinema, Cork. (Courtesy of the National Library of Ireland)

Small lights set into the ceiling of the auditorium were designed to create the illusion that the audience was seated outdoors at night beneath the stars. In the 1930s, a 'cloud projector' beamed images of moving clouds onto the azure-coloured ceiling to further enhance the fantasy.

Schoolchildren queuing to see the film *David Copperfield* at the Savoy Cinema, Cork, 22 January 1936. (Courtesy of the Irish Examiner Archive)

Left: Handbill for the Coliseum Cinema, Cork, c. 1914.
(Courtesy of the National Library of Ireland)

Below: The former Coliseum Cinema, MacCurtain Street, Cork, 2018.
(© Jim Keenan)

The Coliseum Cinema was built on the site of a former iron works at the corner of King Street and Brian Boru Street. It opened on 9 September 1913. It is said that the IRA took control of the cinema during the War of Independence and used the box-office takings to fund their military activities. The cinema closed on 4 April 1964. The last film shown there was *The Man in the Iron Mask*. After it closed the building became dilapidated. In the 1970s, the Department of Posts and Telegraphs used it as a sorting office. It was later converted into a leisure facility.

Coliseum Cinema, MacCurtain Street, Cork, 1915. (Courtesy of the National Library of Ireland)

Coliseum Cinema, MacCurtain Street, Cork, 1966. (Courtesy of the Irish Examiner Archive)

Overleaf: Capitol Cinema, Grande Parade, Cork, 1947. (Courtesy of the Irish Examiner Archive)

C A
SUNBEAM WOLSEY LT
CAFE

PITOL
CAPITOL
CINEMA
HAIRDRESS
CENTRAL BOOT S

Hurst's Picture Palace, Friar Street, Youghal. (Courtesy Roche Collection)

Ruben Hurst, who was born in Scarborough, served as an officer in the British army in the Boer War. He was later stationed in Youghal and married a local girl. After he was discharged from the army, he settled in Youghal and around 1916 he opened Hurst's Picture Palace on Friar Street. The cinema was destroyed by fire in 1935.

Left: Horgan's Picture Theatre, Friar Street, Youghal, c. 1960s. (Courtesy of the National Library of Ireland)

Bottom left: Horgan's Picture Theatre Orchestra, Youghal. (Courtesy of the National Library of Ireland)

Bottom right: Abbey One and Two Cinemas, Friar Street, Youghal, c. 1987. (Courtesy of the National Library of Ireland)

Horgan's Picture Theatre opened on 23 December 1917 – just shortly after Hurst's Picture Palace opened. The two cinemas were situated adjacent to one another on Friar Street. Horgan's cinema was founded by two brothers, Phil and Tom Horgan, members of a well-known Youghal family. In 1973, the 390-seat cinema was subdivided into two smaller cinemas, Abbey One and Two. They lasted fifteen years before closing in 1988.

Above: Regal Cinema, Friar Street Youghal, 1998. (© Jim Keenan) **Below:** Regal Cinema, Friar Street, Youghal, 1980s. (Courtesy of the National Library of Ireland)

After Hurst's Picture Palace burned down in 1935, Ruben Hurst built a replacement for it on a site close to his old cinema on Friar Street, but on the opposite side of the road. He called it the Regal and opened it in 1936 with *The Singing Fool*. It seated 425 and was designed by Messrs Chillingworth and Levie, South Mall, Cork. There was great excitement in Youghal when the film *Moby Dick* was filmed there during the summer of 1954. Youghal doubled as the fictional town of New Bedford and many local people from the town were employed as extras for the film. At its Irish première at the Regal on 26 February 1957, the cinema was packed for the midnight performance as local people flocked to see themselves on the big screen. The cinema was upgraded in 1997 and subdivided into three smaller cinemas. The Regal closed in August 2010.

Above: Regal Cinema, Friar Street, Youghal, 2018. (© Jim Keenan) **Right:** The Regal's main screen and auditorium, 2018. (Courtesy of and © Jörg Köster, Köster Photography Ltd)

The old Regal Cinema lay vacant for seven years before being purchased by Red Barn Construction in 2017. The company spent about €500,000 on redesigning the premises and relaunched them in August 2018. The new owners did a magnificent job of restoring the old building, which now houses two cinemas, a wine bar and café.

Palace Cinema, MacCurtain Street, Cork. (Courtesy of the National Library of Ireland)

The Palace operated as a cinema from 1930 until it closed on 4 June 1988. The last film shown there was *Trains, Planes and Automobiles*. It was purchased by the Everyman Theatre Company and reopened as a theatre in 1990.

Pavilion Cinema, Patrick Street, Cork, 1935. (Courtesy of the Irish Examiner Archive)

The 900-seat Pavilion Cinema with its distinctive Palladian windows cost £30,000 to build and opened on 10 March 1921 with D.W. Griffith's *The Greatest Question*. The most popular film shown there was *ET* which played for eight months in 1983. The Pavilion closed in 1989.

Bandon Cinema, Market Street, Bandon, June 1996. (Courtesy of and © Brendan Golden)

Built on the site of the old Bandon Cinema, which burned down in 1980, the new Bandon Cinema opened on 21 December 1984 with *The Karate Kid* and *Hot Bubble Gum*. Sean Lowney was the proprietor of both cinemas. The new Bandon Cinema closed on 5 June 2000 with the romantic drama *Man in the Moon*.

Broadway Cinema, Mary Street, Dunmanway, May 1996. (Courtesy of and © Brendan Golden)

The Broadway Cinema opened on Easter Sunday, 20 April 1930 with an all-night dance and orchestral music. The hall boasted the largest floor space in the county Cork. However, it wasn't until 3 May 1930 that it opened as a cinema and showed its first film, *Love's Crucifixion*. The cinema was owned by Barnabas (Barney) Deane, and seated 400. Deane emigrated to America around 1900 but returned in 1920. He became blind in old age and management of the cinema passed to his eldest son. The Broadway closed on 5 May 2005 with the adventure comedy *Sahara*.

Stella Cinema, Wolfe Tone Square, Bantry.
(Courtesy of the National Library of Ireland)

Founded by John M. Murphy, the Stella Cinema opened on 26 April 1927. It seated about 500 and the first film shown there was *The Midshipman*. Under the heading 'A rat goes to the pictures', the *Irish Press* reported on 27 October 1955 that 'Women screamed in Bantry's Stella Cinema when a rat got into the parterre during a showing of *Sabrina Fair*.' Early on the morning of 15 July 1942, a serious fire occurred at the cinema which completely destroyed it, leaving only the outer walls standing. It was rebuilt, but by the late 1970s the cinema had deteriorated badly and the roof leaked. It closed for a major renovation and opened again on 25 July 1980 with *The Empire Strikes Back*. The newly-refurbished cinema seated 203 (124 in the stalls and 79 in the balcony). It continued to operate throughout the 1980s, but was put up for sale in 1990. In recent years the building was used as a furniture store.

The former Stella Cinema, Wolfe Tone Square, Bantry, 2017. (© Jim Keenan)

The former Star Cinema, Church Road, Mitchelstown, July 1996. (Courtesy of and © Brendan Golden)

George Henry Sharpe retired from the British army and came to live in Mitchelstown in 1931. He opened the Star Cinema there in 1932 and ran it until he died in 1956. Sharpe's son, Robert, took over the running of the cinema after his father died. The cinema originally seated 450 but that number was later reduced to 300. It was demolished in the 1990s.

Above: Ormonde Cinema, Broderick Street, Midleton, 1998. (© Jim Keenan)
Right: The former Ormonde Cinema, Midleton, 2016. (© Jim Keenan)

The Ormonde Cinema opened in 1946. It was designed by B. O'Flynn and Son, South Mall, Cork. Pat and Kathleen Green ran the 500-seat cinema for twenty-six years. It closed on 1 April 2006. The last film shown there was *Man about a Dog*.

Palace Cinema, Macroom. (Courtesy of the Irish Examiner Archive)

Above left: The auditorium of the Savoy Cinema, Limerick. (Picture courtesy Michael Cowhey and Sean Curtin)

Above right: Savoy Cinema, Bedford Row, Limerick, August 1959. (Courtesy of Sean Curtin and "Limerick A Stroll Down Memory Lane", and Joe Coleman – "House Full" 2014)

The Savoy in Limerick was one of three large, luxurious Savoy Cinemas built for Irish Cinemas Ltd. The other Savoy cinemas were in Dublin and Cork. Limerick's Savoy was designed by Leslie C. Norton in the Art Deco style and seated 1,650. It opened on 19 December 1935 and closed in January 1975. In later years it was used as a venue for concerts. Roy Orbison, Val Doonican and Tom Jones were just some of the many singers who performed there. The former cinema was demolished in 1989.

Lyric Cinema, Limerick, c. 1952. (Courtesy of Sean Curtin and "Limerick A Stroll Down Memory Lane", and Joe Coleman – "House Full" (2014)

The Lyric Theatre (formerly known as the Havergal Hall) was situated on the corner of Glentworth Street and Baker Street. It opened in 1924. The well-known landmark building, which seated about 900, functioned mainly as a first-run cinema, but concerts, operas and plays were also performed there. It closed on 28 August 1976. The building was demolished in 1982.

Picturedrome Cinema, Castle Street, Tralee, 1954.
(Courtesy of and © the Kennelly Archive)

Patrick Coffey, a native of Killorglin, lived in America for nine years before returning to Ireland and opening Tralee's first cinema, the Picturedrome, on 24 February 1914. The premises had previously been a shop. Initially it seated about 300, but in 1940 Coffey expanded the cinema to seat 1,100. When he died in 1952, his family took over the running of the Picturedrome. His daughter, Evelyn, recounted how their family grew up in the cinema: 'Going up the stairs, you'd turn right to go to the cinema and left to go into our house'. On 16 June 1954, projectionist Joseph O'Sullivan was forced at gunpoint to project slides on the screen which were designed to entice members of the audience to join the IRA. In the early 1970s, the cinema was taken over and modernised by Provincial Cinemas. The newly-renovated 493-seat cinema reopened on 15 October 1972. In the early 1980s, the building was converted into a three-screen venue and renamed the Cinedrome. It closed on 16 December 1994 and the building was demolished in May 1995.

HE PICTUREDROME
TWICE NIGHTLY AT
6.45 & 9.0 P.M.
IY 8506

Top left: Abbey Film Theatre, Lewis Road, Killarney, 1971. (Courtesy of the National Library of Ireland)

Modern Irish Theatres Ltd opened their Abbey Film Theatre on 11 October 1970 with the Walt Disney film *Love Bug*. Based in Áras Phádraig, the venue seated 400 people and was also used for live productions.

Bottom left: Lakes Triple Cinema, Killarney, 1977. (© RTE Stills Library)

This cinema was originally Tom Cooper's Casino Cinema, a corrugated iron structure erected around 1932. In 1937, Cooper completed the cinema in concrete. As well as being a successful businessman, Tom Cooper also produced and directed Ireland's first full-length sound feature film, *The Dawn*. The Casino closed in 1973 and was subdivided into three smaller cinemas. The venue was renamed the Lakes Triple Cinema and opened in June 1973. It closed around 1996 and was later demolished. A Cineplex now stands on the site.

The former Tara Cinema, Main Street, Ballylongford, 2018. (© Jim Keenan)

The Tara Cinema opened around 1955. It was founded by Johnny Walsh, a national school teacher and former All-Ireland GAA football player. The cinema seated about 300 people. It closed around 1971.

Left: Kingdom Cinema, Railway Street (now O'Connell Street), Cahirciveen, September 1971. (Courtesy of the National Library of Ireland)

The Kingdom Cinema, Cahirciveen, opened around 1924. It was founded by Charles Troy and Patrick Gilsenan. In later years it was taken over by Jeremiah Breen. The cinema burned down twice in the 1960s. However, on both occasions it reopened. It finally closed in 1974 and was later demolished.

Right: Oisín Cinema, The Square, Killorglin, c. 1990s. (Courtesy of and © Dan O'Shea)

Patrick J 'Duffy' O'Shea and his wife Christine opened their new state-of-the-art Oisín Theatre and Cinema on Main Street, Killorglin, in October 1962. It seated about 600. The first film shown there was *Now and Forever*. On 5 April 1964, it was completely destroyed in a fire. The cinema was rebuilt and went on to show films for another thirty-five years. *Gone with the Wind* and *The Sound of Music* were particularly successful and had extended runs there. In 1984, the cinema closed for a month for a major reconfiguration. It reopened on 27 May 1984 with seating capacity reduced from 600 to 200. The Oisín closed on 4 February 1999. The closing film was *The Negotiator*.

Phoenix Cinema, Dykegate Lane, Dingle, 1996. (Courtesy of and © Brendan Golden)

The Phoenix Cinema was built on the site of the old cinema on Dykegate Lane. It opened in 1937 and seated 600. John Moore was the proprietor from the 1950s to 1974. The well-known West Kerry businessman Michael O'Sullivan took it over in 1979. When the controversial film *The Last Temptation of Christ* was released in 1988, he refused to show it and told the *Kerryman* newspaper 'cinema owners who purport to be Catholics should not show it'. He added: 'I think it's great that people like me in the cinema business can show our colours - we owe enough to the Lord'. The Phoenix has hosted the Dingle Film Festival since 2008. The cinema currently seats about 150.

The former Savoy/New Era Cinema, Main Street, Ballyduff, 2017. (© Jim Keenan)

The Savoy Cinema opened around 1960. It seated 300. It was put up for sale in December 1965 and reopened as the New Era Cinema on 16 October 1966. It closed in the 1970s. Michael Buckley was the proprietor.

Left: The former Arcadia Cinema, New Road, Kenmare, 2012. (© Jim Keenan)

Right: Arcadia Cinema, New Road, Kenmare, 1971. (Courtesy of the National Library of Ireland)

J. Quinlan and P. J. Arthur were the original proprietors of the Arcadia Cinema, which opened around 1947. In 1953, the 323-seat cinema was purchased by Herbie McSweeney and local undertaker John Finnegan. The new owners reconfigured the layout and completely refurbished it. The cinema closed in 1972 but reopened a couple of years later on 14 December 1974. It only lasted a short while before closing permanently.

Above left: Gaiety Cinema, Friar's Walk, Ennis, 1971.
(Courtesy of the National Library of Ireland)

Above right: Burren Film Theatre, Station Road, Ennis, 1971.
(Courtesy of the National Library of Ireland))

Left: The former Mars Cinema, Francis Street, Kilrush.
(Courtesy of and © Alan Souter)

The 850-seat Mars Cinema opened on 16 December 1950. It was owned by Patrick Tubridy. The cinema closed in January 1990.

John Byrnes, owner and operator of the Cinema, Tulla.
(Courtesy of John Byrnes)

The Cinema in Tulla, County Clare, opened in September 1923 and closed in September 1997. It had seating for about 200.

The former Regal Cinema, Davis Road, Clonmel, c. 1990s. (© Jim Keenan)

This venue was originally known as John Magner's Theatre. It burned down in 1919, but was rebuilt in 1921. It later became known as the Regal Cinema. In 1951, Clonmel Corporation bought the well-known landmark building with the intention of using it solely as a municipal theatre. It was renamed Amharclann Chluain Meala. The Corporation sold the building to the Ward Anderson cinema group in 1968. They reopened it as the Regal Cinema on 22 December 1968 with *The Good, the Bad, and the Ugly*. The 850-seat, single-screen auditorium was subdivided into three smaller cinemas in 1988. In 1995, the premises reverted to being a theatre. It lasted about six years before finally closing in March 2001.

Regal Cinema, Davis Road, Clonmel, 1968. (Courtesy of Donal Wylde, *The Nationalist*)

A fire destroyed the Oisín Theatre, Clonmel, on 17 December 1966. (Courtesy of Donal Wylde, *The Nationalist*)

Capitol Cinema, Mathew Avenue, Thurles, 1995. (© Jim Keenan)

The Capitol Cinema originally seated 1,100, but that number was later reduced to 846. It opened on 7 February 1949 with *Unconquered*, starring Gary Cooper and Paulette Goddard. Locals referred to the Capitol as 'the Wan above', to distinguish it from the other cinema in the town, Delahuntys, which they called 'the Wan below'. The Capitol was subdivided into two smaller cinemas in 1979. A third screen opened there some years later. They all closed around 2007.

Estoria Cinema, Galway, c. 1950s.
(Courtesy of Donal Haughey)

Staff of the Estoria Cinema, Galway.

Claddagh Palace Cinema, Lower Salthill Road, Galway, September 1995. (© Jim Keenan)

The Estoria Cinema was built for solicitor Patrick J. Mulligan and his business partner Winifred Eleanor Egan. It opened on 22 November 1939 with the musical film *The Great Waltz*. The 776-seat cinema, which cost £10,000 to construct, was designed in the cubist style by Galway-based engineer Hubert O'Connor. Popular films shown there included *Phantom of the Opera*, *Gone with the Wind* and *They Died with their Boots On*. In the mid-1970s, the name of the cinema was changed to the Claddagh Palace. When the film *Mandingo* was shown there in July 1976, it provoked a protest by the Galway Rosary Crusade. They objected to the sex and violence in the film and recited prayers aloud while picketing the cinema. However, the publicity caused by the protest actually increased box-office takings as people flocked to see the film. The cinema closed on 28 September 1995. Early on the morning of 24 May 1997, the interior was extensively damaged by fire. The premises were subsequently demolished and an apartment block was built on the site.

Gaiety Cinema, Wine Street, Sligo, 1993. (Courtesy of Alec Foley)

The Gaiety Cinema opened on 3 November 1935. The cinema was designed by the Dublin firm Robinson and Keefe, and built by Messrs Kilcawley, Maloney and Taylor of Ballisodare. The cinema seated 1,000. In August 1981, it was enlarged and converted into a three-screen venue. In 1991, an additional fourth screen opened there. The Gaiety closed on 15 June 1997. The building was demolished and a multiplex was built on the site.

Gaiety Cinema, Wine Street, Sligo. (© Alamy)

Left: Estoria Cinema, Teeling Street, Ballina, c. late 1930s. (Courtesy of P.J. Clarke)

Patrick J. Mulligan and Winifred Eleanor Egan founded the Estoria Cinema. The 750-seat cinema was designed by Thomas Francis McNamara and opened on 1 November 1931. At a meeting of the Ballina Urban Council in 1935 councillor Padden suggested that the clerk write to the manager of the Estoria 'requesting that *The Soldier's Song* be played before the programme commences or during the interval, as the people who attended paid no respect to it at the end of the programme only to rush out'. (*Connacht Tribune*, 16 March 1935). The Estoria closed around 2001. The building is now used as a Men's Shed.

Erris Cinema, Main Street, Belmullet. (Courtesy of Seamus Cafferky)

The former Estoria Cinema, Ballina, 2015. (© Jim Keenan)

Left: Crescent Cinema, Bridge Street, Boyle, 18 August 1977. (Courtesy of the National Library of Ireland)

The Boyle Picture Theatre, which dates from about 1922, originally stood on this site. In the 1930s, John Lowe purchased the cinema. In 1939, he expanded and renovated it to accommodate about 600 people. It opened as the Abbey Cinema later that year with the first colour film shown in Boyle, *The Adventures of Robin Hood*. The Lowe family sold the cinema in the mid-1960s to the projectionist Donal Farrell. He ran the cinema for ten years before retiring and selling it on to the Kelly family in 1977. They changed the name of the cinema to the Crescent and opened it on 25 March 1977. The hardware shop adjacent to it burnt down on 8 February 1994 and caused extensive smoke and water damage to the cinema. It never reopened.

Right: The former Royal Cinema, Castle Street, Roscommon, 2016. (© Jim Keenan)

The Royal Cinema opened on 1 October 1948 with *The Naked Truth*, a film-noire starring Barry Fitzgerald and Howard Duff. It was founded by local solicitor Patrick C. Sweeney, T.J. Hanrahan, and J. Rafferty. The cinema seated about 600. A. Robinson was the manager and Joe Casey was the long-serving projectionist. The cinema closed around 1980 and was later converted into a nightclub.

Left: Roxy Cinema, Carrick Road, Drumshanbo. (Courtesy of Mrs Mary Giblin)

Michael John Giblin and members of his family built the Roxy Cinema. Giblin spent many years in New York when he was a young man, but returned to Ireland in the early 1950s. The Roxy opened on Easter Sunday, 12 April 1953 with *Where the River Bends*. It cost £5,000 to construct. Michael Giblin was the manager. His wife Mary was the cashier, Gerry McKeon was the usher and Sean Kielty was the projectionist. The Roxy closed on 30 April 1967 and the building was demolished in May 2004.

The Author

Jim Keenan was born in Dublin in 1948 and began his career as a cartographer at the Geological Survey of Ireland. He lived and worked for many years in Canada, Switzerland and Saudi Arabia, before returning to Ireland in 1984. He was the cartographer at Maynooth University for twenty-seven years and served as a board member of Maynooth University's Governing Authority from 2005 to 2010. A founder member of the Cinema Heritage Group, he was the author of the very successful book *Dublin Cinemas: A Pictorial Selection*. He retired in 2012 and now lives in Dublin. *Irish Cinemas: A History in Photographs* has grown out of his interest in film exhibition and cinema buildings in particular.

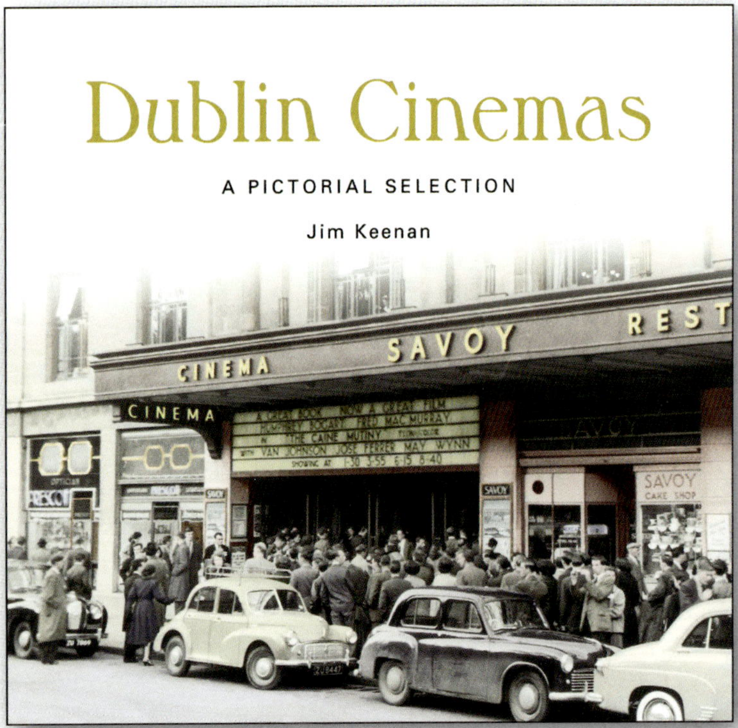